It's What on the Inside

Anthony J. Harris

SKYLIGHT BOOKS

An imprint of Tandem Light Press

Copyright © 2015 by Anthony J. Harris.

All rights reserved. No part of this publication may be reproduced, distributed or transmitted in any form or by any means, including photocopying, recording, or other electronic or mechanical methods, without the prior written per-mission of the publisher, except in the case of brief quotations embodied in critical reviews and certain other noncommercial uses permitted by copyright law. For permission requests, write to the publisher, addressed "Attention: Permissions Coordinator," at the address below.

Anthony J. Harris / SkyLight Books

950 Herrington Road, Suite C128
Lawrenceville, GA 30044
www.TandemLightPress.com

Publisher's Note: This is a work of fiction. Names, characters, places, and incidents are a product of the author's imagination. Locales and public names are sometimes used for atmospheric purposes. Any resemblance to actual people, living or dead, or to businesses, companies, events, institutions, or locales is completely coincidental.

Book design © 2015

Ordering Information: Special discounts are available on quantity purchases by corporations, associations, and others. For details, contact the publisher at the address above.

It's What's on the Inside / Anthony J. Harris — First Edition

ISBN 978-0-9854437-7-1
2014959088

Printed in the United States of America

Acknowledgments

I would like to acknowledge several individuals who directly or indirectly helped me write this book. First, I want to acknowledge the love and encouragement of my wife, Smithenia, who has been there through thick and thin for nearly four decades.

To my daughter, Ashley, who inspired the book and my son, Michael, I love you more than you will ever know. I also want to acknowledge six decades of unconditional love from my late mother, Mrs. Daisy Harris, who, along with my late father, James Harris, Sr., taught me to be a man.

To my brothers, James and Harold, thanks for your much-appreciated brotherly love and support.

I want to express my gratitude and thanks to my editor, Bianca Singleton, for her outstanding editing prowess. I look forward to working with you on future projects. And thanks to several friends and relatives who read and gave me valuable feedback on the many drafts of the book. Thanks to Virginia Mann, Olivia Boggs, Velisa Clark, and LaVada Frazier (my dear mother-in-law) for your help in improving the book.

And finally, I want to thank my publisher, Dr. Pamela Antoinette Larde of Skylight Books, for taking a chance on me and publishing my first children's book. I look forward to working with you again on future projects.

Ashley slowly walked inside the daycare and sat on the floor with her head down. She stayed quiet while she waited for her dad to pick her up. She just wanted to go home and play with her dolls. She did not feel like talking to anyone.

Have you ever felt sad?

Just like he did every day, Daddy picked up Ashley from daycare in his shiny, blue minivan.

And just like he always did when he picked her up, Daddy gave her a big hug and asked, "Did you have a good day, today, sweetie?"

Ashley heard Daddy, but she did not answer him. It was unusual for her to do that. She walked slowly to Daddy's minivan and kept her head down. She was not in the mood for talking.

During the drive home, they passed the field where cows were grazing and the tall, red brick building where Mommy worked. Ashley just looked out the window and didn't say a word..

After Ashley and Daddy came home, she went straight to her bedroom without saying a word. Not to Daddy. Not to Mommy. Not even to her little brother, Michael.

In her bedroom, Ashley took off her shoes and socks and climbed onto her bed so that she could play with her dolls. Her bedroom was a happy place with her favorite colors, pretty pictures on the wall, and toys.

She was still upset, but she did not want to tell anyone why. Do you know why Ashley was so upset?

For a little while, her dolls made her feel better, but she was still feeling a little sad. Ashley decided to talk to someone before dinner. Maybe that would help her feel better.

She walked into the living room and sat down on the couch with Daddy.

"Are you ready to tell me why you are so upset, sweetie?" asked Daddy.

"Yes, Daddy," Ashley said in a soft, sad voice. Tears started rolling down her face.

"Daddy, I don't want to be black anymore."

"Why not, Ashley?" Daddy asked as he grabbed a tissue to wipe the tears from Ashley's face.

"Daddy, Tommy told me today that he doesn't like people with black skin and he doesn't want to play with me anymore.

Tommy is my friend, and his skin is not black like mine. And, Daddy, I'm scared that if I stay black, Tommy won't like me anymore, and he won't be my friend anymore," answered Ashley as more tears rolled down her face.

Daddy did not know what to say. He looked confused and surprised.

Daddy turned to his little girl, picked her up, and put her on his lap. He hugged her tightly.

"Sweetheart, I am so sorry Tommy told you that he doesn't like people with black skin. And I'm sorry that Tommy doesn't want to be your friend anymore because your skin color is black," said Daddy.

Ashley briefly took her thumb out of mouth and said, "But, Daddy, he is my best friend. I like to play with him and he likes to play with me. I won't have anybody else to play with if Tommy doesn't play with me," she said.

I know Tommy is your best friend, and the two of you like to play together and have fun. And I can understand how it would really make you unhappy if he stopped being your friend. But I also want you to know something else that is more important than your friendship with Tommy," said Daddy.

"What's more important than that, Daddy?" asked Ashley.

"First of all, sweetie, your skin color is beautiful. God made it that way," said Daddy.

"But why did God make my skin blacker than Tommy's skin?" asked Ashley.

"He made it that way because he wanted every little girl and boy to have their own one-of-a-kind skin color. And that's why He also gave every little girl and boy their very own hair, their very own eyes, their very own nose, and their very own toes. No one else in the whole wide world has your very same hair, very same eyes, very same nose, very same toes, and very same skin color," said Daddy.

"But, Daddy, your skin color and mine are the same," she said. She placed her arm next to Daddy's arm.
"No, sweetie. They are not exactly the same. Look a little closer," said Daddy.

She looked at her arm and then at Daddy's arm.

"You're right, Daddy. They are different," said Ashley. A smile came to her face.

"So, God likes my skin color, but Tommy doesn't. I don't understand," she said.

"You see, Tommy is a little confused. God doesn't care what color your skin is because God loves you for what's on the inside, not on the outside," said Daddy.

"I don't understand, Daddy. What does that mean, on the inside," asked Ashley.

"It means what is in your heart. It means how you treat other people, how you help them, how you smile at them, and how nice and friendly you are to them. The way you treat other people is more important than the color of their skin. It is what's on the inside that makes God happy," said Daddy as he placed his hand on her face and then on her heart.

Ashley stopped crying. She gave her nose a big blow with a piece of tissue Daddy handed to her.

"God loves you. Mommy and I love you. Michael loves you. Your Grandma Daisy loves you. Your Grandpa Woofie loves you. Your Pop-ee loves you. And your Mom-ee loves you," said Daddy.

Ashley smiled some more. She was starting to feel better.

"But we love you most because of what's on the inside, just like God does. You are fun, funny, helpful, and smart. And you are kind and loving. And we also think that you are a very pretty little girl, with a beautiful skin color. I love your hair. I love your little piggies. I even love your little wrinkly, knuckle nose," said Daddy as he pinched her nose, and squeezed her toes, making her laugh.

"You mean the skin is the outside part and fun, funny, helpful, and smart are the inside parts?" she asked.

"You got it sweetie. And don't forget kind and loving. Remember it is the inside part and not the outside parts that matters to God and to the people who really love you," said Daddy.

"You mean Mommy, Grandma Daisy, Pop-ee, Mom-ee, Michael, and Grandpa Woofie," asked a smiling Ashley.

"Yes, sweetie, we all love you because you are kind, loving, fun, funny, helpful, and smart. If Tommy doesn't want to be your friend anymore, then he will miss you very much. I am sure you will soon find someone else to play with who is just as much fun as Tommy is and who will not care about your skin color," said Daddy.

Ashley jumped down from Daddy's lap and went back to her bedroom to play with her dolls one more time before dinner. She had a great big smile on her face.

She picked up one of her black dolls and said, "You are very pretty, and your skin is pretty just like mine. And I also love you because you are pretty on the inside, just like me."

Ashley would miss playing with Tommy, but just as Daddy told her, she soon found other friends to play with who like her just the way she is, inside and out!

About the Author

Anthony J. Harris was born in Hattiesburg, Mississippi. He was an active participant in the local Civil Rights Movement and has been a champion for ethical leadership for the greater part of his life. Though Dr. Harris has published other books and scholarly articles, *It's What's on the Inside* is his debut children's book. In his previous books, *Fruits of a Disgraced Legacy*, *Gifts of Moments: Being Somebody to Somebody*, and *Ain't Gonna Let Nobody Turn Me 'Round*, he draws from life lessons learned through love, injustice, leadership, and power.

Dr. Harris has been featured on PBS and conducts key note addresses on topics pertaining to the Civil Rights Movement, the educational success of young black males, and leadership. Since 2008, Dr. Harris has served as Professor of Education at Mercer University in Atlanta, Georgia. He and his wife, Smithenia, have two adult children, Ashley and Michael.

To arrange a speaking engagement with Anthony J. Harris, please contact the Tandem Light Press Speakers Bureau at: speakersbureau@tandemlightpress.com. Connect Online: www.tandemlightpress.com/anthonyjharris.html

CPSIA information can be obtained
at www.ICGtesting.com
Printed in the USA
BVHW021716030620
580777BV00002B/62